If you are anything like me, paralyzed at the thought of suffering, then this book will greatly help you overcome your fear. I was truly blessed in reading through this book and the one quote that helped me confront those paralyzing thoughts of losing the things that I cherished is the statement, "We have to be careful of putting ourselves in bondage to our own desires."

– Victor Sholar,
co-author of *Secret Sex War, A Battle For Purity*.

"Shell's personal growth and faith really comes through in a powerful way."

– Quester Adams,
author of *A Meaningful Gift,
Passing on The Richness of God's Love*.

Shelli Ross', "Successful Suffering" is an excellent resource on the subject of fear. Her compelling story of life with multiple sclerosis inspires the reader to find strength to persevere in their own hardships.

– Amber Robinson,
author of *Mercy Rising*

Successful Suffering

PART ONE

Transformation: From Fear to Faith

Shelli Ross

CROSSBOOKS
PUBLISHING

CrossBooks™
A Division of LifeWay
1663 Liberty Drive
Bloomington, IN 47403
www.crossbooks.com
Phone: 1-866-879-0502

Editing by ChristianWritingServices.com.

Scripture taken from the New King James Version. Copyright 1979, 1980,
1982 by Thomas Nelson, inc. Used by permission. All rights reserved.

Scripture taken from the Holy Bible, New International Version®. Copyright © 1973,
1978, 1984, 2010 Biblica. Used by permission of Zondervan. All rights reserved.

Scripture taken from the Amplified Bible, Copyright © 1954, 1958, 1962,
1964, 1965, 1987 by The Lockman Foundation. Used by permission.

First published by CrossBooks 08/12/2011

ISBN: 978-1-4627-0586-3 (sc)
Library of Congress Control Number: 2011914084

Printed in the United States of America
This book is printed on acid-free paper.

Any people depicted in stock imagery provided by Thinkstock are models,
and such images are being used for illustrative purposes only.

Certain stock imagery © Thinkstock.

CONTENTS

FOREWARD

Many people find inspiration and courage from hearing the testimonies of saints who maintained unwavering faith in the midst of heart-wrenching adversity. As for me, I always come away challenged because of my own spiritual inadequacies. There are things in life I don't want to let go of, privileges that I cherish, a wife and four sons whom I love dearly. And to imagine having these blessings taken away from me at any moment can be paralyzing. But the one reality we are confronted with is that the Bible promises that Christians will suffer. And as much as I would prefer for the Lord to bring trials that don't affect the things I cherish, yet I must continually remind myself that if God loved me so much that He would cause His own Son to suffer a bloody death on the cross, then He is guided by that same love when He brings suffering in my life. If the death of His Son was the means of bringing me into a relationship with Him, then suffering is the means of experiencing the awesomeness of that relationship. Therefore, when God takes away a gift in trials it is for the purpose of replacing it with a greater gift, more of Him.

And there is no one that I know on a personal level whose life embodies this truth more than my dear sister Shelli Ross. There were things in her life that she did not want to let go of, privileges she cherished, and the Lord in His wisdom removed those gifts and replaced them with a greater one. It was John Knight that said, "God is often pleased to use disability as a protection against drifts into the fog of lukewarmness". Shelli's multiple sclerosis was her protection against the drift into the fog of success that can often cause lukewarmness. And it is her testimony of this experience coupled with her ability to accurately apply precious truths from God's Word that qualifies her to write this book, "Successful Suffering".

If you are anything like me, paralyzed at the thought of suffering, then this book will greatly help you overcome your fear. I was truly blessed in reading through this book and the one quote that helped me confront those paralyzing thoughts of losing the things that I cherished is the statement, "We have to be careful of putting ourselves in bondage to our own desires". I thank God that He saw fit to protect Shelli from wasting her trial through self-pity or bitterness, because you would not have in your hands a precious resource of encouragement and instruction on how to be successful in your suffering. May our Lord and Savior Jesus Christ be magnified in using this book to help you seek comfort in Him in your season of suffering (2 Corinthians 1:3-5).

Pastor Victor Sholar
Main Street Baptist Church
Lexington, Kentucky

DEDICATIONS

To my daddy, Edward Ross, the man who exemplified no fear in the way he loved his wife. He showed resolute faith and commitment to the word of God in the way he raised his three daughters. Thank you dad!

To Bruce (Stan) Klein, thank you for demonstrating the absence of fear and fullness of faith when you assumed the position of a humble servant by praying for me on bended knee, with many tears.

INTRODUCTION

*My brethren,
count it all JOY
when ye fall into
diverse temptations (trials)
James 1:2*

Over the years God has blessed me with the opportunity to walk through high waters and overflowing rivers, ferocious fires and vicious flames, and the proverbial "valley of the shadow."

Those were blessings? you might ask. Look at it this way: All these natural phenomena represent trials. The purpose of the flame is to purify, and the water is designed to cleanse. After each of my own trials ended, I discovered I hadn't drowned or been burned. Because God is faithful and because God is a promise keeper, his children, in a spiritual sense, will not drown or be burned in the midst of their trials.

I base this claim on the Word of God and my own personal experiences. After all, the Lord guarantees in Isaiah 43:2 that he will be with us as we traverse the waters, rivers, fires, and flames of life. God also promises that although the fires of adversity and trials test our faith, we will bring him glory when we endure (1 Peter 1:6–8). God does not intend for trials to destroy us but, instead, to strengthen us.

The Lord has never promised a life devoid of hard times. We *will* get wet from the water, and we *will* get hot from the flame. But we can rest assured that God is sovereign and always in control of our adversities. Perhaps your trials and hard times might seem larger than life, and you may feel as though you are drowning in a flood or burning at the stake—but that's not true! That's a lie from the enemy—Satan himself!

My heart's desire is that this book will help you and me together to understand why God allows trials and to know how he expects us to endure them. My experiences have taught me that I had numerous misconceptions about suffering. One of them was thinking that I had to get through difficult times by myself, depending on my own limited strength. While I struggled in a feeble attempt to successfully overcome each adversity as it came, the Lord sat by patiently, saying in his still, small voice, "Let me lead you.... Let me carry you.... You can't do this without me."

Before I share with you the lessons I learned from the Word of God, I will give you a glimpse of some of my fire-and-water experiences, times when I went through purification and cleansing appointed by the Lord. Although these times were hard for me, I now see the blessings in the midst of the pain. I have learned many lessons and grown closer to my Lord and Savior in the process. I have discovered that every trial is a process—and every trial has a purpose.

CHAPTER 1

Fire and Water

*M*y childhood was characterized by the stability of a Christian home. My parents loved the Lord and taught all of us about the great love and selfless sacrifice of the Lord Jesus Christ. The second of three daughters, I learned early on that Jesus paid the debt for my sin by giving his life on the cross and that he was buried in a tomb and was resurrected three days later. When I was six years old, I gave my life to Jesus Christ, trusting him as my Lord and Savior. During my time at a Christian school, I continued to learn more about Jesus.

My junior high and high school years were spent in a public school and followed the same peaceful path. I was a goal-oriented honor roll student with very high expectations. Athletically inclined, I developed a sincere love for sports. I played basketball and ran track throughout junior and senior high school. After graduation, I enrolled at the University of Illinois with a scholarship in the field of electrical engineering.

Little did I know that my childhood years—when I first met Jesus, grew to know more about him, memorized Bible verses, and learned the stories of the Bible—would prove to be my preparation for the trials that would later be an intricate part of my life.

The trials

I was nineteen years old and in the second semester of my junior year of college when I was diagnosed with multiple sclerosis (MS). MS is a degenerative nerve disease that renders the body unable to properly transmit signals from the brain to various other parts of the body. This disease can affect vision, speech, hearing, level of energy, or mobility— or all of the above in addition to other functions not mentioned. MS affects people in different ways; it is a disease that seems to customize itself to each person.

Majoring in electrical engineering required intense hours of study. Since this particular program attracted the best students from across the country, the level of competition was stiff and stressful. I developed the habit of studying until 2:00 a.m., then getting up in time to attend my eight o'clock class six hours later. But with the MS, the continual stress on my mind and body began to affect me in several ways. First I discovered that my vision was being compromised. My gait when walking soon began to follow suit.

As my vision and mobility became more challenged, I was forced to alter my activities and habits. As I said before, I had been very athletic and had continued my involvement while in college, teaching aerobics and weight lifting. But I soon discovered that instead of being healthy, these activities were actually detrimental to my health. I began to wonder, *Is MS supposed to be the "good" that the Lord has in store for the child that he bought with a very precious price?* (1Peter 1:18-19).

My type A personality demanded, among other things, that I stay up late and study. You see, I could accept nothing less than an A for a grade (I was to find out later that anything above a C was acceptable!). Of course, I was the only one who could make the grades and a degree a reality—or so I thought. Not once did I consider that my God was able and willing to help. I needed him. He knew I was a sheep in need of a Shepherd. He did not need me to help him do great things in my life. In his own time, the Lord demonstrated to me exactly what he could do—without my assistance!

Provision

By now I was in my fifth year at the U of I, needing just one class to graduate. It was supposed to be an easy class, but it was taught by a new professor, and he was hard!

My vision had deteriorated to the point where I could not see well enough to read the blackboard. In addition, my level of fatigue had increased, and walking was becoming more difficult. Physically, my body was drained. It seemed as if everything was going against me. But that's when the Lord stepped in and began to fight the battle I thought I might lose.

Although Professor "C" (that's what we'll call him) was a very demanding teacher, I watched the Lord soften his heart. Right away he discovered I was unable to see the blackboard even though I sat in the front row, so he looked for another student to take notes for me. When that failed, he gave me *his* notes. Then he began staying past his office hours to explain the material to me in more depth. But that wasn't all. After breakfast with his family on Saturdays, he devoted approximately two hours at a coffee shop with me to review everything he had taught that week.

Even with all that extra preparation, however, Professor C was still concerned that my visual deficiency would compromise my performance on the final exam. But as the day of the three-hour test approached, he became confident that I was able to verbally recount knowledge of the material and knew it well enough to pass the course. Then to my surprise and amazement, he instructed me not to come to his final exam and granted me a C in his class anyway! These are things that flesh and blood cannot do. Only the Spirit of the living God could orchestrate a plan like this.

I completed my undergraduate studies because the Lord was doing things that only he could do. Whatever made me think the Lord needed my help? Only God can change a man's heart. I know without a doubt that I would never have completed that class or touched the professor's heart without the intervention of almighty God. I couldn't have convinced him to devote that much time and attention in assisting me to pass his class, but then I didn't have to. God did it.

Protection

God had only begun showing his sovereignty and wisdom in my life. The time finally arrived for the graduation ceremony. So much had happened during the past five years, and I was insistent upon marching in with my classmates to receive my diploma. But on graduation day, as we were lining up to walk into the stadium, the Lord sent a graduate student my way who was officiating in the ceremony.

After informing me that I could not make the walk, he took me down an elevator to the floor of the stadium. I was led to a chair on a dark stage, and there I sat and watched as the graduation spectators filed into the stadium. Then I began crying. I had worked so hard and persevered so long in the face of this illness to complete this degree, and I could not understand why the Lord would not allow me to walk with my classmates. It never crossed my mind at the time that he was actually protecting me.

Then I looked up. My graduating classmates, around three thousand of them, began descending down a seemingly never-ending flight of steep stairs, characteristic of athletic stadiums. Then the light dawned. Most likely I would have fallen and possibly been responsible for the injury of others if the Lord had not been merciful and gracious enough to protect me in my ignorance.

Instead, the Lord positioned me on a stage where all could see what he had done. He was glorified! It wasn't what Shelli had done: He alone was responsible for my having a degree in electrical engineering, and he alone was responsible for me sitting on the stage and not walking down those never-ending stairs. All by himself, he alone was worthy of all the glory!

Direction

At the beginning of that last year at the university, I had been graciously given the opportunity to apply to graduate school. Heidi, the secretary in the engineering office, said she would type the application and send it to the school of my choice. I didn't want to go to grad school, but what did I have to lose by sending off an application? So I applied to Wright State University in Dayton, Ohio, and then forgot all about it.

Before graduation I started trying to map out the course my life would follow. First, I had to decide where I would work. I had turned down a few jobs, but I still had an opportunity left with a well-known company in Chicago. However, I discovered the position would require me to travel a lot, work in the field, and climb poles. I knew that this job wasn't a match.

I began to earnestly pray and ask the Lord what direction I was to take. Up until this point, I had just assumed my direction would include a career in electrical engineering. With no other opportunities left, I finally began to think that maybe the Lord had another plan.

I ran into a couple of guys graduating with me, and they told me they were not going to work. They said they weren't ready for corporate America. Instead, they had decided to go to grad school. Then I remembered that application I had sent off to Wright State. I hadn't heard anything from them, so I immediately contacted the school. The master's degree program was small and normally filled up quickly, but there was room for one more. In March I received an acceptance letter.

Even more amazing, I was also awarded a scholarship that included living expenses of $1,000 per month! The Lord saved that position and the finances because it was a part of his plan for my life. The Lord has a way of sometimes working *and* leaving his signature as well. Finally, the ultimate signature mark from the Lord was found in the type of program to which I applied: *Rehabilitation Engineering.*

Looking Back

I had wanted to be an engineer for a long, long time. In fact, as a twelve-year-old seventh grader I was selected to go to an engineering camp. When I returned from camp, I was often asked if I aspired to an engineering career. My response would be, "I plan to major in electrical engineering and then to work with handicapped people." (I know that the word *handicapped* is not politically correct today.) I now realize the Lord had placed that desire on my heart. At the time I did not personally know anyone who was disabled. I certainly had no suspicion that one day I was going to experience disabilities first hand.

This idea of working with the disabled stayed with me until I started working as an engineer during my summer internships at college. But when I began to reap the financial benefits that came with being an engineer, my focus shifted.

College came, and when MS began to compromise my health, I was referred to the Department of Rehabilitation Services at the U of I. There I received the assistance and accommodations needed to help me complete my classes and obtain a degree. This is when the Lord got my attention and reminded me of the desire he gave to a twelve-year-old girl to work with the disabled. The advent of MS and the ensuing struggles it brought with it caused me to refocus and remember what I had aspired to do as a seventh-grade student.

At the U of I Rehab, not only did I receive needed accommodations, but I also worked with a professor who designed computer aids for people with visual disabilities. This professor was instrumental in directing me toward the grad school that I was set to attend. However, because of my limited mobility and compromised vision, I was hesitant to go. That's when the Lord led me to Hebrews 10:38: "Now the just shall live by faith; but if anyone draws back, my soul has no pleasure in him." That verse sent me to grad school despite my fears.

Lessons learned at grad school

The Lord once again showed me his favor, this time at Wright State. Completion of the rehabilitation engineering program took one year for full-time students. In addition, the number of students enrolled in the program had decreased from ten to five and ultimately ended with two. As a result, the course work remained the same, but the competitive nature of the program and the high level of demand from the instructors subsided. This reduced my stress level, allowed me to get the rest I needed, and encouraged me to spend more time focused on my Lord.

During that year in Dayton, I learned so much about the Lord and witnessed him repeatedly working on my behalf. When I arrived, I didn't know a soul, but as I attended classes and performed my daily tasks, I watched as the Lord ushered people into my life. I thought he was providing them just to do those tasks that challenged me, but I soon realized that he was multi-tasking! Not only were others there to help me—I was also there to help *them*.

As far as I can remember, not one of the people he sent into my life during this time knew Jesus as Lord and Savior. Knowing this made it my responsibility to tell them that Jesus Christ died on the cross for them so they could know him as Savior and Lord and live eternally with him.

While I learned how to use engineering to work with the disabled, my most important lessons were in developing a boldness to tell others about Jesus—lessons with results that will last for eternity. The Lord gave me the power to be bold in my witness for him. I gained more knowledge about the character and ways of my God. I learned to exercise discernment and to recognize his voice. I learned to study his Word and live my life for him alone. These are the lessons that prepared me for the opportunities I would have in the future to live wholeheartedly for Christ and share the gospel.

A Master of Science degree in biomedical engineering with a specialty in rehabilitation is just icing on the cake. Although I did not realize it then, now I see that my Lord is the cake. My Lord is the one I want. Icing is nice, but it isn't very good without the cake. As a matter of fact, too much icing will make us sick! We need the cake to balance it all out. Without the presence of the Lord to add balance and give perspective to our blessings (the icing), we run the risk of getting sick.

Off to work

I spent approximately three months back home in Indianapolis prior to heading for Illinois and my first job in the field for which I had been trained. But I think my body was so excited to have a break, it decided to hibernate! As a result, I needed a cane to walk by the time I started the career to which the Lord had called me. In addition, multiple sclerosis had more dramatically affected my vision: I was now legally blind.

So I started a job working with disabled clients as a disabled person myself—but I absolutely loved it! I trained blind and visually impaired individuals to use computers, using special software that provided speech output and/or enlarged print. I was also given the opportunity to provide worksite modification recommendations for physically challenged clients. I share what I did not to brag, boast, or toot my own horn, but to show the goodness and infinite wisdom of God. Let me explain.

Because I had disabilities of my own, the Lord was able to work through me to touch hearts that might have been untouchable by a totally healthy individual. I had the advantage of being able to identify with the struggles of every client with whom I worked. They couldn't say to me, "You don't understand." This proved a blessing because in many situations the door then opened for me to share the good news of Jesus Christ's sacrifice. If I had been totally able-bodied, these opportunities might not have come along as easily; but the Lord had a plan in it all. Since he is always looking to save lost souls, my purpose was to share the gospel message of his love with co-workers, clients, and anyone else who would listen.

Once again overexertion soon took its toll, a result of extended working hours and excessive physical activity. For instance, I chose to walk to work when the weather was cooperative. Walking was a lot of fun and good exercise but probably wasn't the wisest thing to do on a daily basis. My office was only one block away, but a hill made the trip suspenseful. If the path had been level, there would have been nothing to it, but I had to make my way down that hill to get there. Whenever I started down, I never knew if I was going to walk or slide down.

Although I never injured myself walking, the disease progressed and my physical condition worsened. I had only worked for a little more than a year and a half, but I couldn't continue any longer. Hoping that a long-overdue, much-needed break would allow my body to heal and recover, I resigned from the job I loved. I did not know it, but my time as a rehabilitation engineer had come to a close.

But my God, as always, had a greater plan.

Back home

I returned home on March 25, 2000. After living on my own for seven years, I had a big adjustment to make! I did not return singing and dancing; I came back out of obedience to the Lord. I had to. It simply would have been unwise to get a roommate and look for a job just to maintain my independence. With a questionable, ever-changing physical condition, the Lord directed me back to Dad and Mom.

I praise God for giving me a father and mother who loved the Lord so much that they were able to love me as I struggled to adjust to my disabilities. Being a very independent, do-it-yourself type A personality can make life difficult for anyone who has an illness, be it mental, physical, or spiritual. Looking at my circumstances from a different perspective, I now see that the Lord has been doing a perfecting, maturing work on the entire family. I cannot speak for my family and friends, but I can share with you what he has done in *my* heart.

Now that my life had seemingly come back to where I started, there were questions that I wanted the Lord to answer. Certainly he was under no obligation to respond, but I had become obsessed with understanding why this adversity had invaded my life. I was not yet ready to accept my disappointments by faith, so I struggled to trust and believe he had my best interest in mind. I wrestled continually with the fact that he was allowing multiple sclerosis to attack me because it would ultimately work out for my good (Romans 8:28).

So I began praying and asking the Lord to take me to the next level in him. I thought if I prayed for that, I would move up and out of these circumstances. But I thought the next level meant blessings, independence, and a life without the issues that had come with this adversity.

Returning home and resting was supposed to usher in a season of restoration and healing; that was what made sense to me. But my reasoning did not correspond to the mathematics of heaven! After being home only four months, my balance was worse, my muscles became very tight, and I required a wheelchair to travel anywhere away from home and a walker around the house to get from room to room. My career, my independence, and my mobility were gone.

The result

I had never dreamed I'd go from teaching aerobics to needing a wheelchair. My heart was so broken, discouraged, and weary that I was driven to draw closer to my God. I cried, called his name in prayer, and searched his Word for answers. I became involved in intense, inductive Bible studies, and the time I spent in prayer increased dramatically. As I drew closer to him, the Lord drew closer to me (James 4:8).

Yes, my thinking *was* wrong. I learned that the next level is not higher but deeper—deeper into fellowship with Jesus Christ. The next level meant nothing less than greater intimacy with the One who gave his life as the payment for my sins, and the Lord continued to take me even deeper.

I cannot take credit for the spiritual growth in my life. All of the glory goes to God. I know that if he had not orchestrated the events in my life, I would not have voluntarily taken the time to cultivate my relationship with him.

CHAPTER 2

It's Definitely Coming!

*T*he idea of suffering is foreign to many Christians. In fact, most of us do all we can to avoid it at any cost. That is why trouble, trials, and tribulation can catch us unaware. We are shocked and surprised when we are allowed to go through "fiery" trials, even though the Lord told us that trouble would be an inescapable part of life: "In the world you *will* have tribulation" (John 16:33, emphasis mine). An earnest, sincere look into the Word of God will reveal that hard times accompany each beat of your heart. In other words, if blood runs through your veins, trouble is close by. Either it has just left, is on its way, or it is all around you at this very moment!

This may sound like doom and gloom, but it's not intended to be depressing or disheartening. Encouragement is found in knowing that God is with you in adversity (Isaiah 41:10). Because of his love, God has planned for all his children to come through adversity victoriously. The Lord tells us trouble will come to prepare us for its arrival. Along with his admonitions, the Lord gives us rules for warfare so we can be steadfast and stand firm when times get hard and *nothing* makes sense.

This book focuses on the response to adversity that is pleasing to the heart of God. Through the lens of the Word of God, we will seek to understand the acceptable response in the midst of trials. Our motive is to learn how he expects us to go through and conquer life's adversities.

Trouble shows no partiality

No one has a choice concerning the advent of trials, but we do play a part in deciding to allow the Lord to resolve them. Along with the promise of trouble, however, comes the promise that our Lord is near and ready to do a wonderful work in us—if we will only allow him to.

An old spiritual song simply yet eloquently describes trouble, its effect, and the biblical solution:

> Trouble in my way;
> I have to cry sometimes;
> Jesus, he will fix it after 'while.

Many times in our lives we all will have an opportunity to sing this song. The only reason we won't sing these lyrics is if we're not willing to let Jesus fix our problems and deliver us from our troubles. According to the Bible, trouble is in everybody's "way" (or life), but not everybody is willing to let Jesus mend their broken heart and shattered dreams. Even though we are sometimes willing, at other times we still struggle to trust him, thinking that we have a better solution.

The surety of trouble

> "Man is born to trouble, as the sparks fly upward" (Job 5:7).

> "Be not far from me, for trouble is near" (Psalm 22:11).

> "Do not think it strange concerning the fiery trial which is to try you, as though some strange thing happened to you" (1 Peter 4:12).

Just as the sparks from a fire go up the chimney, know that troubles will be a part of life. These times may be painful and frustrating, but they are neither strange nor extraordinary. Remember, you are not the only one going through times of testing. Trouble is everywhere. It is experienced all over the world, not just in America. It's not just in *your* home, *your* city, or *your* state.

Rest assured that while you are going through troubles, trials, and adversities, the Lord is doing a marvelous work. During these times, God is close by your side. He is working in you, in those around you, and in your circumstances. With the same certainty that you believe that trouble is an unavoidable part of life, believe that God is in control and working on your behalf. These facts are absolutes: Trouble is coming; God is in control; and God is at work in the midst of your troubles.

What the Lord promises to do

- "Many are the afflictions of the righteous, but the LORD delivers him out of them all" (Psalm 34:19).

- "May the God of all grace, who called us to His eternal glory by Christ Jesus, after you have suffered a while, perfect, establish, strengthen, and settle you" (1 Peter 5:10).

- "When you pass through the waters, I will be with you; and through the rivers, they shall not overflow you. When you walk through the fire, you shall not be burned, nor shall the flame scorch you" (Isaiah 43:2-3).

We can learn a lot about God in the midst of our trials. In the book of Psalms we are frequently told that troubles are numerous, but regardless of the struggle or the type of problem, the Lord will deliver us. Deliverance comes in various shapes, sizes, and colors. Peter's first epistle reveals that the Lord is maturing his children, and trials are the means he uses to accomplish this end. In Isaiah forty-three we learn that the child of God is never alone in a trial because the Lord is always there. Knowing this brings comfort.

Water, rivers, fire, and flames represent the intensity. The Lord is always there and controls the intensity of every trial. He maintains his sovereign control in the midst of life's adversities. He will complete his perfecting work in each one of his children through the fires, flames, rivers, and waters of life.

The Lord will deliver from trouble. Yet we may find it difficult to trust him when his deliverance is delayed and we must wait for him, especially when he acts in a way contrary to our expectations. As children of God, we must understand that he *will* come in his perfect time and deliver in his perfect way—not our time or our way.

If we expect to experience the joy and peace that come with the Lord's deliverance, we must accept *everything* that comes from his hand, including the delays. We must know that everything he gives and all he does will work for our good (Romans 8:28).

We have briefly looked at the inevitable advent of trouble, trials, and adversity. We have also seen God's promises, which give us comfort in the midst of the troubles of life. At this point, we should be asking two questions: *How do I endure these times?* and *What response will please the Lord?* The remainder of this book is devoted to finding the answers to these questions by studying examples found in the Scriptures. Some will be good enough to imitate—some will not. There will be some successes—and some failures.

CHAPTER 3

Our Response

The fearful response

hy are we so afraid to attempt the task the Lord calls us to accomplish—with his power? To go to the places he sends us—when he has promised to be there beside us? To endure trials—when he guarantees victory? To bear a burden—when he has promised to sustain us? Sadly, when circumstances look insurmountable and victory seems impossible, we easily lose sight of everything we know about God.

Why is that? If we're honest with ourselves, we know we often use this kind of reasoning: "If I can't do it (or "If I can't do it my way"), it can't be done!"

At the same time, God reminds us, *You can't do it; but it **can** be done! So let **me** accomplish this impossible task through you. I promise you this: It will work for your ultimate good and my glory.*

Yet continuing in our utter disbelief, we go our own way, never trusting God. We seemingly prefer to believe that he doesn't know what is best for his children. Instead, we listen to Satan's lies.

There are many problems with this mind-set. First, we fear things, people, and our own insufficiency. We don't feel we have the strength to measure up to the challenges they represent. That's an *unhealthy* fear. But a *healthy* fear of these things is the fear of having to face them alone, without the Lord. The best tasks to attempt are those the Lord calls us to finish. Successful completion is impossible without the intervention of our almighty God. When we come to the end of ourselves and our fears lose their influence over us as we focus on God, the Lord steps in. When he intervenes, the battle is won, and the victory is sweet!

A second problem is our failure to exercise faith. It is hard to trust someone you don't know. Or, is it that it is hard to trust someone you can't see? Know this: It is better to have faith in the God you can't see with the naked eye than to trust in sinful man whom you can see. Oftentimes, faith is defined as believing without seeing. Another definition could be "seeing through God's eyes." But even better, faith is taking God at his word and believing everything he says.

It is possible to believe that a trial will work out for good. The biggest problem for you and me is that we don't see how that can happen. Many times our problem lies in the object of our focus. When we focus on the wrong person or only on our circumstances, our faith will falter because it has been misplaced. God's Word must be honored as absolute truth. When we cannot see how bad circumstances will be resolved, we need to hold firmly to everything he has said. We *must* learn to trust his Word!

There remains one last issue: our knowledge of our Lord and Savior Jesus Christ. We all may have heard about his love, sovereignty, power, and mercy, but the knowledge he wants us to have is an intimate knowledge gained through experience. This intimacy is first cultivated in time spent praying and reading the Bible. Then when we see God act on our behalf in a personal way, our relationship with him is strengthened. It makes Jesus real, our intimacy with him real, and gives credence to his promises because we witness him working in and through our lives. The result of knowing the Savior in a deeper way (not superficially) decreases fear and increases faith.

In case you haven't noticed, these three issues overlap. If we know him better, we trust him more. If we trust him more, we exercise faith in the midst of our trials. When we exercise faith in the midst of trials, God eliminates the fear that attempts to dominate our response. On the other hand, our fear, lack of faith, and lack of an intimate knowledge of the character of God will keep us from pleasing the Lord because "without faith it is impossible to please Him" (Hebrews 11:6). God, our Father, is ready and willing to enable us to live victorious lives of faith!

The proper response

Jesus talked to his disciples about the certain advent of trouble in their lives just before he was betrayed and crucified. John 16:33 records that Jesus told them that trouble was definitely coming, but he also told them how they should respond and why:

These things I have spoken to you, that in Me
you may have peace. In the world you will
have tribulation; but be of good cheer, I have
overcome the world.

Several of the Old Testament patriarchs demonstrated
the response that pleases God, while others illustrated
the response that breaks God's heart. These testimonies
have impacted my walk with the Lord and taught me
the importance of trusting God while walking through
turbulent times in my life. As a result, my faith has
increased and fear has dwindled as I have focused on
God.

This doesn't mean I never fear, nor does it mean my
faith is never shaken. But now I have a history with the
Lord. My own past experiences in trials and testings have
confirmed that God really does strengthen my faith and
empowers me to respond appropriately. When I fall down,
he picks me up, and I am strengthened and made ready
for the next task. And every time I respond in faith, he is
glorified and victorious!

The choice

Every child of God has a choice to make: Will I function
in fear or will I function in faith? All born-again believers
will be required to make this decision repeatedly. It is not
about how we feel but what we know, who we know, and
our obedience to him. As we grow in Christ, our response
to trouble will begin to follow the victorious blueprint
given by Paul, the apostle, in 2 Corinthians 4:8-9:

> We are hard-pressed on every side, yet not crushed; we are perplexed, but not in despair; persecuted, but not forsaken; struck down, but not destroyed.

In these verses Paul outlined what the Lord desires our attitude to be as we face the battles. Fear comes from focusing on circumstances that are out of our control. In the heat of the battle, amidst adversities and unpleasant circumstances, we must move ahead with this mind-set: No fear! All faith! This attitude will only be rooted in us when we completely rely on the Lord as Paul did.

"No fear, all faith" does not have anything to do with the feelings and emotions that bombard your heart and mind. It has everything to do with the way you function. You might be fearful. You may be confused. But you have to decide now that you will function based on the Word of God, the character of God, and the promises of God.

"No fear, all faith" is not about feeling—it is a choice! It's about how you perform in the conflicts of life. Successful suffering is birthed when you make the choice not to function according to your fears, but to walk by faith.

Food for thought

> For whatever is born of God is victorious over the world; and this is the victory that conquers the world, even our faith.
>
> —1 John 5:4 AMP

- What troubles or adversities have invaded your life?

- Whom do you trust?

- Are you functioning based on your fears or on your faith in God?

CHAPTER 4

Fear

Peace I leave with you, My peace I give to
you; not as the world gives do I give to you.
Let not your heart be troubled, neither let it
be afraid.

—John 14:27

These words of our Lord Jesus give assurance that God
never intends for us to suffer the ill effects of trials.
But fear can paralyze the children of God and rob them
of the wonderful blessings that God desires to give.

The Lord gives the commands "do not fear" and
"do not be afraid" more than 350 times in his Word.
When we disobey these admonitions, fear dominates
our thoughts, our attitude, and our actions. When fear
dominates, it can cause us to stop any forward motion,
which stifles our progress. We will be unable to make a
decision, think clearly, or hear the still, quiet voice of the

Lord. In addition, fear will create a strong resistance to change, feeding the inability to let go of the things and people the Lord has called us to release. Fear will cause us to forfeit our walk of obedience.

The first step that needs to be taken in the journey toward successful suffering is to minimize the fear-dominated response. Knowledge of the character of God can keep his children from being controlled by fear. The Lord never intended for us to live life being suffocated by terrifying circumstances. He continually reassures us that he is in control and has planned a good outcome (Romans 8:28).

In fact, tribulation and adversity provide the most fertile soil for growing in our knowledge of God and developing an intimate relationship with him. In perilous times, God's children will be driven to his heart. Adversity makes us more aware of our need for him and creates a growing desire to know him more. We can know *about* God by reading his Word and observing him work in the lives of other saints. But we can *experience* him as he puts out our fires and drains the overflowing waters of our lives.

It is the troubles of life that set the stage for the Lord's character to be put on display. Fear, on the other hand, will shift our focus away from God and magnify our circumstances. When the stage has been set by adversity, we can choose to be more attentive to God. On this platform we recognize our desperate dependence on the Lord, and it is there that we crave to know him. Consequently, adversity gives birth to the circumstances that cause the believer to seek after his or her Lord.

While the platform of adversity is ripe to display the character of God, it is also set to display our response to these testings. Since God is omniscient (all-knowing), he is not shocked by his child's response—good or bad. Adversity is designed to show us believers the response that God already knew would come. We may be surprised at how we respond, but there is no excuse for not knowing the response that God desires from his children. A response guided by faith—not fear—gladdens the heart of God.

In Isaiah 41:10, the Lord tells his children not to fear:

> Fear not, for I am with you; be not dismayed,
> for I am your God. I will strengthen you, yes,
> I will help you, I will uphold you with My
> righteous right hand.

Notice that along with that command, he gives five assurances that should serve to short-circuit the fear-dominated response:

1. He is with his children.

2. He is their God.

3. He will strengthen his children.

4. He will help his children.

5. He will hold his children with his righteous right hand.

Be encouraged! Know that this promise is for every born-again believer. If you have given your life to Jesus

Christ and acknowledge him as your Lord and Savior, fear can be your defeated foe. The choice is yours.

Fear

The Hebrew word for *fear* is *yare* (yaw-ray'). It means "to make afraid, to frighten, to dread, to revere."[1] When we are afraid of or frightened by someone or something, we hold that person or thing in a position of respect. Our response and reaction reveal the truth. The fearful response is often masked by an attempt to control the people or circumstances close at hand. The desire for control is often born out of a fear of change. When our efforts to control do not yield the desired results, our energy can transform into anger—all because of fear.

If *fear* were an acronym, the following words would describe it well: False-Evidence-Appearing-Real—FEAR. Many of our fears originate with a lie. The starting place for that lie is normally the mind. Or the lie can start in the mind-set and words of a close friend or relative with the best of intentions. Lies can be believable, especially amidst our turbulent circumstances.

When we analyze the starting point for our fears, we find they often begin with these simple words: *why, what if, maybe,* and *how.* When trials first strike, we are tempted to resort to questioning or rationalizing: *Why is this happening? What if I lose my job? Maybe they don't like me. How will I ever get over this?*

Often the conclusions we come to are lies implanted by the enemy of our souls and do not come from the Lord. Some of the lies we accept sound like this: "God can't." "God won't." "God doesn't know what is happening in my life." "God doesn't care." One of the most effective lies is this: "I have to solve this problem alone because the Lord isn't going to help me." You may ask, "How do I know these are lies?" Simply because these statements are totally contrary to the Word of God!

Looking through our own eyes encourages these questions and doubts. But by looking into the Bible, the answers to some of our questions are given, the lack of the validity of others is seen, and our confusion, stresses, and doubts can be settled. One perspective breeds fear; the other cultivates faith in God. Jesus is *the* answer and he is our peace.

Sometimes God gives detailed answers for a specific problem, but not always. Oftentimes he withholds the details, wanting his children to trust him (Psalm 62:8, Proverbs 3:5). God commands us to trust, not to fear. But his command is often taken as a suggestion when it is, in fact, a mandate. When pressure comes, it is easy to rationalize and think that it's acceptable to worry and doubt. However, we know that Jesus tells us, "Do not be afraid; only believe" (Mark 5:36). Those words are the words of the Creator of the ends of the earth. They are not to be dismissed simply because we fall back on what comes naturally.

Fear causes many saints to shrink back instead of moving forward in faith. According to Hebrews 10:38, 39, the Lord is not pleased when fear causes his children to shy away from his will. Hebrews 11 gives ample evidence that a walk of faith is pleasing to the Lord, but "without faith, it is impossible to please Him" (v. 6).

Everything God has commanded us to do, he will strengthen us to do. The problem comes when the believer neglects to trust him. Trust may not prevent fearful situations, but trust will protect the believer against functioning in fear. When we function in fear, we have failed our God.

Our faithlessness breaks the heart of God. Fear is an assault to his character. When controlled by fear, the child of God shows that he or she does not believe God will do what he promised. In effect, the believer is saying that he or she believes God is a liar. Without a proper knowledge of God's character, the snares of adversity, hostile circumstances, and fear of an unfavorable outcome can take precedence over his Word.

Along with the knowledge of God's character, believers must have the faith to be obedient to his commands. Fear can only be replaced by faith when we ingest the Word of God by hearing and reading (Romans 10:17) and allow the Holy Spirit to cast it out (Philippians 2:13).

Exposing fear

Because fearfulness is not a sought-after character trait, both men and women will disguise fear. Often believers do not acknowledge fear as a worthy opponent that wars against pleasing God. Therefore, they are not aware that fear is cowering behind an action or emotion considered more acceptable to society. This is a tactic developed by Satan himself. Being so easily beguiled by the enemy will cause us to function in fear and prevent us from pleasing God.

Fear is deceptive and hides easily behind other emotions. Here is a big secret: Fear is oftentimes afraid to stand alone. Often we do not acknowledge that fear is hidden behind the best of intentions. Because fear is an undercover emotion and prefers to hide, it is important to identify its disguises. By identifying fear's hiding places, we can expose it and choose to replace fear with faith. Only then will we be equipped to function properly as Christian soldiers, please God, and war against the enemy.

The following are some potential hiding places for fear. If one of them is present in your life, it may be a legitimate concern or safeguard; these are merely suggestions. Only you and the Holy Spirit know your heart, but be honest with both yourself *and* the Lord.

Attitudes that can mask fear:

- I am just using wisdom.
- I am just exercising caution.
- I don't want to look like a fool.
- I don't want to be hurt.
- I might fail due to a lack of …
- I'm fine.

Take note: "I" is the main character when fear dominates.

Actions that can mask fear:
- isolating yourself from others
- denying the truth concerning a situation or problem
- depending on your wisdom instead of God's

- avoiding confrontation
- attempting to run from the presence of God
- endeavoring to control circumstances and other people
- getting angry

We allow ourselves to walk in fear when we fabricate answers to questions that cannot be answered by man, or we don't believe God is attentive to our lives and our problems. There are times in our lives when the only answer we have is "But God …" If we desire to be satisfied with that answer, we have to be able to fill in the blank. We must know our God, intimately. We must know his character. We must know him well enough to focus on him instead of focusing on the situation that creates an atmosphere of fear. Independent of the Lord, we would be unable to live fearless lives. But with him, "All things are possible" (Mark 10:27).

Fear is a major cause of disobedience. Although God promises repeatedly to protect and provide for his children, we often neglect to do God's will because we are afraid that stepping out in faith will be to our detriment. Everyone experiences fear, but never allow fear to keep you from being used by God. The fear-dominated response is indicative of the absence of faith. Because faith is absent, such a response corresponds to spiritual failure. It is spiritual failure because without faith we cannot please God (Hebrews 11:6).

Simply being a child of God will not remove the circumstances that lead to a fear-dominated response. Because we are fallen creatures, we will sometimes make the wrong choice when given the opportunity to choose between fear and faith. When we neglect to renew our minds (Roman 12:2), we will react based on our fears and forfeit the joy that comes from functioning in faith. Instead of "no fear, all faith," we will operate according to the opposite combination: "all fear and no faith." To avoid a life driven by fear and the path that leads to defeat, we must consistently renew our minds, know and trust God's character, and remember his promises.

It may be a long and painful process as the Lord matures his children to a level where they instinctively choose faith over fear. In times of testing, the Lord will often use the people and things that are close to our hearts in order to rid our hearts of the fear that dominates. The testing will work out for our best. It doesn't always look like it, but Romans 8:28 assures us it is true: "We know that all things work together for good to those who love God, to those who are the called according to His purpose."

As we become trusting and obedient, the result will be an abundant reward from the Lord.

Food for thought:

> Fear not, for I am with you; be not dismayed, for I am your God. I will strengthen you, yes, I will help you, I will uphold you with My righteous right hand.
>
> —Isaiah 41:10

- How have you responded to the adversity in your life?

- Do you trust God?

- Is your fear disguised? Identify its disguise.

CHAPTER 5

The Attitudes of Failure

Principle: Ingratitude is the attitude that opens the heart and lets in worry, doubt, and unbelief.

hen looking with sincerity into the mirror of the Word, many people see their own reflection in the faces of the unbelieving Israelites because the Israelites portray a heart condition that reflects all sin-sick souls—the heart of unbelief.

Unbelief begins to grow when we display ingratitude for the blessings the Lord has already given. When the attitudes that characterize doubt are not crucified, they lead to the loss of contentment and thankfulness. The Lord has shown repeatedly that discontentment and ingratitude are unhealthy responses that allow unbelief and fear to control the heart.

Murmuring and complaining reveal ingratitude and a discontented attitude. This "attitude of ingratitude" prevents the child of God from enjoying the Lord's blessings—not because God changes his purpose and plan, but because we neglect to recognize and appreciate what he gives us and does for us. Focusing on the wrong things results in ungrateful hearts.

Let's inspect the emotions and attitudes within the hearts of the Israelites as they journeyed from Egypt to the Promised Land. By doing so, we can see when and how unbelief and fear are able to take root and grow. This is a valuable lesson to learn, for if we stop the growth of the seeds of ingratitude when they are first planted, we can avoid developing attitudes that cause us to disregard God's blessings. Then we will avoid sick hearts characterized by incessant murmuring and complaining. Most importantly, we will escape the consequences of unbelief that cause the Christian to fear.

The Israelites

In God's dealings with the children of Israel, he taught them that he is a God who protects, provides, and judges. Repeatedly the Lord showed his power and goodness on behalf of the Israelites. He delivered them out of slavery and bondage in Egypt, parted the Red Sea, provided manna and quail for food in the wilderness, and led them with a cloud by day and a pillar of fire by night. The Lord performed these miracles because he promised to meet all of their needs and desired to satisfy some of their wants. But despite all he had done, the Israelites complained— and God was displeased.

> Now when the people complained, it displeased the LORD; for the LORD heard it, and His anger was aroused. So the fire of the LORD burned among them, and consumed some in the outskirts of the camp.
>
> —Numbers 11:1

Read it again! It's somewhat difficult to swallow the fact that a God as loving as ours who had protected them and provided all that they needed would respond to the complaining of his children with such harsh judgment. Why then did he do it? Because their complaining was a habit, a way of life, and it revealed their selfish, faithless, and thankless hearts. Without faith, they displeased the Lord (Hebrews 11:6). He wanted them to trust him wholeheartedly. He wanted to be their all, their sufficiency, their "enough." Sadly, even though they had witnessed God perform many miracles and work wondrous signs, he still wasn't enough.

Instead of remembering how the Lord had freed them from bondage in Egypt, they chose to remember the food they had eaten as slaves. Then, in the grip of ingratitude and discontentment, they began to long to return to Egypt. As a result, the people complained. The manna wasn't enough, so they cried for meat to eat—meat that would only fill their bellies temporarily (Numbers 11:4). They were willing to fill their stomachs for the moment at the cost of starving their souls and displeasing the Lord.

Nevertheless, the Lord gave them meat in addition to manna. He did indeed allow them to fill their stomachs, but he told them the meat would not be enjoyable and would make them sick (Numbers 11:18-29).

But God, in his faithfulness, still supplied all of their needs (and some of their wants as well) as he continued moving them toward Canaan. The Lord had given the children of Israel everything they needed to reach their destination because he loved them, but because their hearts were hard and devoid of faith in the Lord, they were never satisfied—God was not enough.

Ingratitude, unbelief, fear, and discouragement had overwhelmed the children of Israel. Their ungrateful hearts had blinded them, and because of this they were unable to praise and worship God. Soon their murmuring and complaining would prevent many of them from experiencing the fullness of God's blessing, the Promised Land.

Still murmuring and complaining

Amidst all of the grumbling and complaining, the Lord remained committed to fulfilling his promises to Abraham and his descendants. In Numbers 13:2 the Lord said, "Send men to spy out the land of Canaan, which I am giving to the children of Israel." Two facts make this statement important: God was going to give them a preview of the blessing, and God said that the land would be given to them. This means that it was a sure thing. In a sense, the land they would see was already theirs.

God had once again demonstrated his grace and mercy by allowing them to see their promised homeland. But after he told them to inhabit the land, they balked at his command, saying, "Let us send men before us, and let them search out the land for us, and bring back word to us of the way by which we should go up, and of the cities into which we shall come" (Deuteronomy 1:22). They still didn't trust God Almighty to lead them!

The Lord then told the children of Israel about the bounty of the land he was giving them. His intentions were that his people never fear, and he planned to fight on their behalf. The Lord wanted them to focus on the blessing ahead, not the battle.

Twelve men, one from each of the twelve tribes, were chosen to act as the spies. But their mission started out on the wrong foot immediately. As they entered the land, they could choose what to focus on—God's power and promise or their own limited strength. Most of them chose to focus on their own strength. In their mind, success or failure would be determined by what they saw when they went in.

It was a matter of belief. Of the twelve, only two had a proper focus and insight as to what the Lord could do. Ten men trusted only what they saw, and they saw a task that could not be accomplished through human efforts. Two men saw the possibilities through God's eyes, and they remembered everything God had done and promised to do.

After forty days the spies returned to the Israelite camp and reported what they saw: "We went into the land to which you sent us, and it does flow with milk and honey! Here is its fruit. But the people who live there are powerful" (Numbers 13:27-28 NIV).

When the people began complaining after hearing this news, Caleb, one of the two, responded, "Let us go up at once and take possession, for we are well able to overcome it" (v. 30).

However, the fearful ten discouraged the children of Israel once again by reporting that this was a land that devoured its people, and that the Israelites were like grasshoppers compared to the inhabitants of Canaan. "We can't attack those people; they are stronger than we are" (v. 31). The report was true, but their focus was wrong.

The children of Israel had a choice to make: Who would they believe—God or man? Unfortunately, they made the wrong choice. Here is their response following Caleb's courageous words:

> And all the children of Israel murmured against Moses and Aaron, and the whole congregation said to them, "If only we had died in the land of Egypt!…Why has the Lord brought us to this land to fall by the sword?"… So they said to one another, "Let us select a leader and return to Egypt."
>
> —Numbers 14:2-4

Wrong move! Remember that the Lord had delivered the Israelites *from* Egypt because he heard their cry for deliverance (Exodus 3:7–8). He then continued showing his compassion, mercy, grace, and love by giving them everything they needed to complete the journey to their new home. On their part, the Israelites had chosen to show their appreciation by failing to recognize all he had done for them.

The two who stood for the Lord, Joshua and Caleb, appealed to the children of Israel one last time:

The land we passed through to spy out is an exceedingly good land. If the LORD delights in us, then He will bring us into this land and give it to us, "a land which flows with milk and honey." Only do not rebel against the LORD, nor fear the people of the land.

—Numbers 14:7-9

Sad to say, that plea didn't help. For all their beseeching, the Israelites threatened to stone them.

The children of Israel did not lift up their eyes and look at God and remember all that he had already brought them through and blessed them with. In their hearts, they were ungrateful. With the wrong heart attitude they chose to look at their own limited strength, the size and strength of the Canaanite men, and the fortified cities of the Promised Land. Because the Israelites neglected to look to the Lord, they compared the strength of the Canaanites to their own weakness and insufficiency. They did not view the strength of the Canaanites in contrast to the power of God. For these reasons they were not willing to obey God and take the land the Lord wanted to give them.

Before becoming too critical of the Israelites' fear and rebellion, ask yourself how you measure up in a similar walk of faith. All children of God need to take the advice given in Numbers 14:7-9. We must not rebel against God nor fear the obstacles before us, and we must believe that *everything* God has promised to give us is good. Like the children of Israel, we also have a choice to make. We must decide whose eyes we will look through and what we will focus on. Scripture admonishes us to lift up our eyes (Isaiah 40:26; Psalm 123:1) and look to Jesus (Hebrews 12:2).

The Lord's response

All of this constant murmuring and complaining from the Israelites grieved the heart of God. Then when the mass of people threatened to stone the two men who stood for the Lord, his anger burned. Their ungrateful, unfaithful attitudes, along with hearts filled with unbelief and fear, ignited the wrath of the Lord.

The Israelites earlier had been so disillusioned and unfocused that they wished they had died in Egypt or in the wilderness. Therefore, just as the Lord had given them their hearts' desire when freeing them from slavery in Egypt, he decided to give them the desire of their hearts once again. He spoke to Moses and Aaron:

> How long shall I bear with this evil congregation who murmur against Me? I have heard the murmurings which the children of Israel murmur against Me. Say to them, "As I live," says the LORD, "just as you have spoken in My hearing, so I will do to you: the carcasses of you who have murmured against Me shall fall in this wilderness, all of you who were numbered, according to your entire number, from twenty years old and above. Except for Caleb the son of Jephunneh and Joshua the son of Nun, you shall by no means

enter the land which I swore I would make you dwell in."

—Numbers 14:27-30

Have you ever heard the saying, "Be careful what you ask for—you just might get it"? What happened to the Israelites is a prime example. All the children of Israel were the intended recipients of the Lord's covenant with Abraham. But because of the condition of their hearts, a vast number would not receive the blessings or the promises of the Lord. They wandered for forty years in the wilderness and died without seeing the land promised so many years before.

The Promise Keeper

After passing judgment, the Lord announced his plan to bless the descendants of the Israelites: "But your little ones, whom you said will be victims, I will bring in, and they shall know the land which you have despised" (Numbers 14:31).

A child of God must remember that God is a promise-keeping God. The Lord made a covenant with Abraham regarding his descendants inheriting the land of Canaan. Although the older, complaining Israelites would not see it, their children would inherit everything the Lord had promised to give.

We can rest in knowing God will keep his promises despite the sinful nature of his children.

Have we made similar mistakes and missed the blessings the Lord wanted to give us? Have we caused him to find someone else to bless because our hearts were ungrateful and unbelieving?

Lessons learned from the Israelites

Psalm 78 recalls the Israelite's journey, the sad story of God's goodness and their ungratefulness. Verse 22 explains the reason for God's anger: "Because they did not believe in God, and did not trust in His salvation."

Although God was gracious and patient with them, his judgment was severe because his mercy had been so abundant. Let the Lord's mercy in the lives of his people move you to be more sensitive to the mercy he showers on all of us.

We serve a merciful and gracious God who longs to bless his children. But we must understand that he is also the righteous Judge, for our heavenly Father is just and holy. Our sin and unbelief grieve his heart and will prevent us from living the abundant life.

Because the hearts of the children of Israel were not right before the Lord, unbelief, bitterness, and ingratitude reigned. Do not allow fear and unbelief to reign in your heart. Instead, learn well the lessons that he has taught us through the children of Israel:

- Remember God's promises: "For all the promises in him [Jesus] are yes" (2 Corinthians 1:20).

- Obey: "Walk in all the ways that I have commanded you, that it may be well with you" (Jeremiah 7:23).

- Never fear: "It is I; Do not be afraid" (John 6:20).

Food for thought

> Take heed, brethren, lest there be in any of you an evil heart of unbelief.
>
> —Hebrews 3:12 KJV

- What attitude of failure have you identified in your adversity (unbelief, ingratitude, discontentment, etc.)?

- Do you murmur and complain? About what?

- What is the condition of your heart? Have fear and unbelief taken root?

- Identify everything you do not entrust to God.

- What is God's perspective on the thing(s) you fear?

CHAPTER 6

Why We Fail

Principle: When worry, doubt, and unbelief control our thoughts, emotions, and actions, fear has gained a foothold.

We closed the last chapter with a solemn warning against unbelief. When we allow our actions and attitudes to be governed by fear instead of faith, we will not please God. The reasons we fall short of God's standard are often mistakenly attributed to unfavorable circumstances or other people. *The reality is that we tend to overlook our own shortcomings while failing to recognize the areas in our heart that need to be conformed to the image of Jesus Christ.* This glorious transformation will only be realized when we are able to trust our Father wholeheartedly and without reservation.

By failing to trust God, believers open their hearts to be consumed with worry, doubt, and unbelief. Then, as these attitudes overwhelm the soul, they are headed toward a fear-dominated response to their adversity. And the result of this mind-set casts a shadow of doubt on the character of God. To successfully endure trials, it is essential to eliminate the fear-dominated responses. This can only be done by returning to the Word of God in humility and gaining his perspective on fear.

Because faith is rooted in the believer's knowledge of God's character, our worry, doubt, and unbelief become devices that will slowly and subtly destroy faith. But when the believer identifies and exposes the places where these mind-sets reign in his or her life, the uncertainties surrounding the character of God will diminish, and fear will no longer control the heart and mind.

Biblical proof

There are many examples in the New Testament where Jesus taught the principles of implicit trust in God and the peril of fear. Examples also abound where his disciples gave in to worry, doubt, or unbelief. The following three passages from Matthew's gospel will help us gain an understanding of how lack of trust leads us away from God and into fear.

1. Talking to his disciples about the kingdom, Jesus said,

    Therefore I say to you, do not worry about your life, what you will eat or what you will drink; nor about your body, what you will put on. Is not life more than food and the body more than clothing? Look at the birds of the air, for they neither sow nor reap nor gather into barns; yet your heavenly Father feeds them. Are you not of more value than they? Which of you by worrying can add one cubit to his stature? So why do you worry about clothing? Consider the lilies of the field, how they grow: they neither toil nor spin; and yet I say to you that even Solomon in all his glory was not arrayed like one of these. Now if God so clothes the grass of the field, which today is, and tomorrow is thrown into the oven, will He not much more clothe you, O you of little faith?

—Matthew 6:25-30

Observe:

- Worry gives a faulty perspective on what is important in life.

- Doubting God's ability to provide causes worry.

- Worry is an irrational attempt to act as God and change circumstances.

- Doubt and worry replace faith and encourage fear.

Putting it all together

Matthew 6 paints a good picture of the battle between having faith in God and relying on ourselves to work it out. This scenario highlights the tendency we have to trust ourselves more readily than we trust God. When worry, doubt, and unbelief come into the picture, we are prone to fear. In this passage we are presented with the lack of food, shelter, and clothing. Fear leads us to attempt to solve our own problems before we cry out to the Lord. We soon forget the Proverb that instructs the believer to "trust in the LORD with all thine heart; and lean not unto thine own understanding. In all thy ways acknowledge him, and he shall direct thy paths" (Proverbs 3:5-6 KJV).

Being presented with a problem we can solve can be a direct affront to our faith. Instead of trusting God to meet our needs, we trust ourselves to figure it out. Some have even resorted to illegitimate means to remedy the deficit they are facing. God has promised to meet all of our many needs (Philippians 4:19). So worrying indicates that fear is our motivation.

That played out differently in my life, yet the principle was the same. I wasn't worried about food, shelter, or clothing: I was worried about being unable to walk. At the age of twenty-five, when I was no longer able to get around, I asked the Lord to restore my ability to see well enough to drive and restore my energy level so I could walk well enough to teach aerobics.

After a few months of waiting, I was motivated to do what I could. For me, that meant eating right, taking the latest medicine, exercising, and getting any raw vegetable I could get my hands on and putting it in liquid form so I could drink it. I became so consumed with eating right so I could walk again that I lost my focus on *Jesus Christ*.

We have to be careful of putting ourselves in bondage to our own desires. It is important to make sure that our efforts are not contrary to God's will for our lives. We all have needs, but Jesus wants to be the one to fill them. As we depend on him to meet those needs, our faith grows and we learn to trust him more.

2. Now when He got into a boat, His disciples followed Him. And suddenly a great tempest arose on the sea, so that the boat was covered with the waves. But He was asleep. Then His disciples came to Him and awoke Him, saying, "Lord, save us! We are perishing!" But He said to them, "Why are you fearful, O you of little faith?" Then He arose and rebuked the winds and the sea. And there was a great calm. And the men marveled, saying, "Who can this be, that even the winds and the sea obey Him?"

—Matthew 8:23-27

Observe:

- Viewing circumstances outside God's sovereignty creates an environment for worry, doubt, and unbelief to flourish.

- The disciples gave in to doubt about Jesus' ability to deliver them from the storm.

- The disciples did not believe that Jesus was aware of their trouble.

- Their doubt and unbelief led to fear, which indicated a lack of faith.

Putting it all together

The disciples knew they had no control over the water, the waves, and the wind. When the Lord did not come to their aid when they thought he should, they panicked. Although they had believed in Jesus, the Son of God, they neglected to recall the attributes of his character. The *man* Jesus was sleeping in the storm—the *deity* in Christ was aware of the storm. He saw their pain and fear.

God tested the disciples' faith on yet another occasion on the sea. As they sat alone in a wave-tossed boat, Jesus came toward them, walking on the water. Frightened first by the storm and now this fantastic appearance of the Lord, Jesus spoke. A.B. Simpson writes,

> The blessed Lord condensed it all into one single message of eternal comfort spoken to the disciples on the Sea of Galilee, "It is I, be not afraid." He is the antidote to fear; He is the remedy for trouble; He is the substance and the sum of deliverance. We should, therefore, rise above fear. Let us keep our eyes fastened upon Him; let us abide continually in Him; let us be content with Him. Let us cling closely to Him and cry, "Therefore will not we fear, though the earth be removed, and though the mountains be carried into the midst of the sea" (Psalm 46:2). [2]

Do we differ from the disciples? When we endure adversity and the Lord delays deliverance, don't we question his character? How many times do we discount

God's love, his goodness, and his sovereignty when we're in an adverse situation? We must remember that God is always the same. He doesn't change, and no matter how difficult our circumstances may seem today, he still loves and still delivers. Be encouraged today that the God who created you and Jesus who died on the cross have not changed.

3. And when they had come to the multitude, a man came to Him, kneeling down to Him and saying, "Lord, have mercy on my son, for he is an epileptic and suffers severely; for he often falls into the fire and often into the water. So I brought him to Your disciples, but they could not cure him." Then Jesus answered and said, "O faithless and perverse generation, how long shall I be with you? How long shall I bear with you? Bring him here to Me." And Jesus rebuked the demon, and he came out of him; and the child was cured from that very hour.

   Then the disciples came to Jesus privately and said, "Why could we not cast him out?" So Jesus said to them, "Because of your unbelief; for assuredly, I say to you, if you have faith as a mustard seed, you will say to this mountain, 'Move from here to there,' and it will move; and nothing will be impossible for you. However, this kind does not go out except by prayer and fasting."

   —Matthew 17:14-21

Observe:

- There was a young boy possessed by a demon.
- The disciples could not heal him.
- Jesus was able to heal him.
- The disciples asked Jesus why they were unable to heal him.

This account is straightforward, and the lesson is easy to understand—right? Not necessarily. I spent a few days reading and rereading this text in an effort to interpret it and apply it to my own life. Sadly, we have the habit of leaving out the Holy Spirit—the most important person—when attempting to interpret the Word of God and apply it to our personal lives. Only when we look to the Lord for his guidance can he interpret his Word and speak to our hearts. For this to happen, it is also essential for us to leave behind all preconceived notions and ideas.

With this in mind, let us take an in-depth look at the Lord Jesus' response to the question posed by the disciples.

Jesus' response

After Jesus drove the demon out of the child, his disciples asked him why they were unable to do the same thing. Jesus' response (vv. 20-21) revealed to them that the true problem did not reside with the external man but with the heart. It was not that they lacked man's knowledge, education, or wisdom—the problem was that their hearts were full of what *they* could do and not what the Lord desired to do through them.

Jesus narrowed their problem down to a lack of faith (unbelief) and a lack of dedication. Their problem rested in their relationship with Jesus and a lack of dependence on the Almighty. The cause for fear does not reside in the externals or with circumstances—it is within our hearts. It begins with unbelief, which creates a comfortable environment for fear.

Jesus' response to the disciples is often his response to our failures as well. Sadly, the same hindrance that prevented the disciples from being successful in casting out the demon still hampers many Christians today. Nevertheless, the choice is yours, and the choice is mine. Like the disciples, we have the opportunity to choose our response to the difficult situations in our lives—to respond in either fear or faith. With the option to choose comes the freedom to select the consequences.

Unbelief, fear, and dedication

Jesus brings out three points in his response to the disciples. They seem to overlap, and each one of them carries consequences—some positive, others negative. We will take each one of these issues and look at the outcomes.

Jesus first addressed their unbelief. The Greek word for unbelief used in Matthew 17:20 is *oligopistia*.[3] It is defined as "littleness of faith, lack of faith." From the definition of the word and the context in which it is used, we begin to see the inverse relationship between unbelief and faith: more faith, less unbelief; no unbelief, all faith.

Throughout Scripture we see many causes and consequences of unbelief. In Matthew 13:58 Jesus did not work mightily in the midst of the people because of their unbelief. Mark 16:14 attributes unbelief to a hard heart. In 1 Timothy 1:13 the apostle Paul links his unbelief prior to his conversion to ignorance, and the author of Hebrews links unbelief to an evil heart (Hebrews 3:12).

The cause of an unbelieving heart is the evil rooted in the heart of man. The consequences that come from having an unbelieving heart could be eternal. If unbelief keeps someone from accepting Jesus Christ as Savior and Lord, the consequences become eternal. Those who have accepted Christ experience temporal consequences. Our unbelief will lead to the fear that causes pain and prevents us from experiencing the perfect will of God and his blessings.

When Jesus told the disciples that some things are only conquered by prayer and fasting (v. 21), he shined light on their lack of dedication and preparation. True prayer and fasting require a lot of energy and a lot of time. But there are times when we attempt to win the victory solo, and any attempt to go it alone has a direct correlation to our devotion to the Lord.

Like the disciples, most believers prefer not to waste any time. Instead we choose to solve our problems our own way, independently, according to our personal schedule. "Quick and in a hurry" is our preferred method of operation, not God's! When self-sufficient confidence is our attitude, we fail. We must be dedicated to the Lord, not simply to finding a solution to our problem. Focus is the key, and our focus must be on the Lord. Failure is imminent every time something or someone else takes the Lord's place of being number one. Look at the disciples. They failed to conquer a demon: We fail to conquer our fears.

In the passage from Matthew 6, worry and doubt resulted in an insufficient amount of faith. The second rebuke of "little faith" that we examined, found in Matthew 8, was a result of unbelief made evident by the fear that controlled the disciples' behavior. An in-depth look in Matthew 17 shows that the believer's victory is dependent on the believer's faith. That passage also reveals that faith relies on a proper relationship to and dependence on the Lord. The inverse relationship between faith and fear is obvious in these passages.

We have gleaned truth and now understand why the disciples failed. We must also apply this truth to our personal circumstances.

Matters of the heart

Ultimately, it is a matter of the heart. When fear, worry, or unbelief reign in our life, we have a heart problem. Now that we have looked at the relationship, the cause, and some of the consequences of these three enemies of faith, we can begin to do a heart check.

In the previous chapter we studied one of the best biblical examples of utter unbelief—the chronicled journey of the Israelites from Egypt to Canaan. In the Israelites we saw a lifestyle of unbelief, attitudes of unbelief, and the price they paid as a result of their unbelief. Unbelief creates an environment in which fear is nurtured and cultivated. In the next chapter Abraham will demonstrate how fear can grip our hearts and cause us to make irrational decisions.

Praise God, we have not been left to fight this battle against fear alone. In his mercy, he has provided the remedy for our fears. God's goodness contrasted with the sin nature of the Israelites and Abraham teaches us both how and how *not* to walk through our fire-and-water experiences. God continues to be good and faithful as believers today struggle with the same fallen nature.

Think about it

God desires that we short-circuit worry and unbelief so that fear has no conduit in which to run. When fear is deactivated, faith in God can flourish. How much control does fear have in your life? Let go of all of your worries. Reject everything that opposes believing God. Know that there is no security to be found in our strength and efforts. Functioning in fear—the reason for our failure—can be traced back to the heart governed by worry, unbelief, and doubt.

This is the time that we must remember the character of God and his promises. Troubles and perilous times do not validate unbelief, worry, or fear. We have to look beyond our circumstances and set our minds on the right things (Philippians 4:8-9). We must count his Word and his promises to be true despite the appearance that our troubles and problems are winning the battle. Suffering can only be successful when we choose to focus on God and his promises.

Food for thought

> For God has not given us a spirit of fear, but of power and of love and of a sound mind.

> —2 Timothy 1:7

- Are you doubting or worried? About what?

- Are your doubts or worries consuming you? Explain how and why.

- Are you giving in to fear? Describe how.

CHAPTER 7

When We Fail

Principle: We must press on despite our unbelief, knowing that God does not change his plan because we fail.

*H*ow does the Lord respond to his children when they function in fear? His response will vary from one situation to another, but it doesn't change because of variations in his standard, character, or holiness. Jesus is the same yesterday, today, and forever. His standard remains the same all the time for all his children. But in his sovereignty and wisdom, he chooses the best way to work out his plan for our individual lives. The differences are found in comparing God's plan with our lifestyle. The question we need to ask ourselves is *Do I habitually function in fear?*

Studying how our Lord has worked in the lives of other believers is important. For example, reading the accounts of the Lord's activity in the lives of saints in the Old Testament brings comfort and hope because what the Lord did for saints then, he is willing to do for saints today.

> For whatever things were written before were written for our learning, that we through the patience and comfort of the Scriptures might have hope.
>
> —Romans 15:4

When Old Testament practices are compared to New Testament principles, God is proven to be steadfast and faithful. He does not, cannot, and will not change.

Looking at the successes, failures, and God's providential care in the life of Abraham, the man called "friend of God," gives me great comfort, for God's character is revealed through the way he worked in Abraham's life.

How I can identify with Abraham! My life has not always demonstrated total faith and trust in the Lord. I, like Abraham, didn't handle the questions I had for God properly. When I didn't understand what God was doing, I didn't lie, but I did rely on self-will and what I could figure out. Praise God that what the Lord determined to do in our lives was planned before the earth was formed. We can be encouraged because what the Lord has planned to do will come to pass! There is absolutely nothing we can do to mess it up.

Abraham failed on many occasions. He initially struggled to exemplify fervent faith and total trust in

God. Nevertheless, God's faithfulness remained, and his love, plan, and promises never changed.

God desires to perform the same way in our lives today. As we observe God's response in the midst of Abraham's failures, we will be encouraged to watch him work in our lives. As you examine how God worked in Abraham's life, ask the Holy Spirit to confirm to your heart which principles and precepts apply directly to your successes, failures, troubles, trials, and adversity.

God's plan and God's promises

God chose Abraham (called Abram until God made a covenant with him [Genesis 15]) and called him for a specific purpose (Genesis 12). He promised Abraham five things: 1) to make a great nation of him; 2) to bless him; 3) to make his name great; 4) to bless all the families of the earth through him; and 5) to give his descendants the land God would show him.

With these five promises there was only one command Abraham had to obey—*Go!* The Lord instructed Abraham to leave the land of Ur and travel to a place he would show him. But before God would show Abraham where that land was located, he had to step out of his comfort zone.

Let's look at the odds Abraham was dealing with. Maybe I should say, let's look at the *God* Abraham was dealing with. Five-to-one odds are not bad (actually, they are excellent when serving the faithful, promise-keeping God!). All the Lord told Abraham to do was to go. God had a plan for Abraham's life and gave him a glimpse of all he planned to do. The only thing God didn't show Abraham was how he was going to do it.

Later on Abraham would be tested again in a similar fashion. He would be told to do something but given nothing about the in-between steps of getting to that point. But the faith he exemplified on that occasion had its roots in his obedience at the beginning of his journey.

Let's go over the steps leading up to Abraham's successes and failures in faith, just so we're all on the same page. The Lord had instructed Abraham to leave his hometown and his family and go to a place he would show him—Canaan. So Abraham departed Ur with his wife, Sarah, his father, Terah, his nephew, Lot, and all their servants. Instead of going directly to Canaan, Abraham and his people stopped in Haran and resided there until Terah died. When his father died, Abraham got the same command from God: "Get out of your country and from your relatives, and come to a land that I will show you" (Acts 7:3).

After Abraham and Sarah obeyed the Lord by leaving Ur, God showed Abraham the land promised to him— the land of Canaan. He also gave Abraham insight as to how he would multiply his descendants. Then the Lord promised that those descendants would come directly from Abraham's body and outnumber the stars in the sky (Genesis 15). Later on God promised that the first descendant would be the fruit of Sarah's womb (Genesis 17). By that time Sarah was nearly ninety and Abraham was ninety-nine, and they had no children. To Abraham, the promise looked impossible.

Note that the Lord only gave Abraham the information pertaining to how he would fulfill the promises *after* Abraham exercised obedience and left Ur. If he hadn't obeyed, he never would have experienced the blessings of God. Even so Abraham succumbed to unbelief and doubt and made mistakes when traveling to Canaan and waiting for the son that God had promised. Praise God that those mistakes did not change God's plan! Even when Abraham chose to function according to his fears, God remained faithful.

Functioning in fear: the mistakes

We should praise God that he recorded these times of Abraham's doubt, fear, and unbelief. They serve as a reminder that the Lord knows we are like flowers and grass that wither (Isaiah 40:7). He knows we are fragile and prone to mistakes, failure, and fear. That certainly does not give us a license to sin—instead, it provides a reason to worship and praise him.

Abraham's failures underscore the compassionate and understanding nature of God. Let's look at two mistakes and then the great success of Abraham's life to glean principles from each of them and apply those principles to our own lives.

First mistake

After Abraham, Sarah, and Lot arrived in Canaan, a famine struck the land. Abraham decided to take his wife and go to Egypt to look for food (Genesis 12). But before they ever got there, fear and doubt overtook him. Thinking of the beauty of his wife, the strength of the Egyptians, and his own insufficiency, he told Sarah to lie and say she was his sister (a half-truth, which is the same as a lie). He feared that because of her beauty, the

Egyptians would kill him to gain Sarah. He never took into account God's power and that *he* was more than able to protect them. Nor did he reflect on the promises God had made to him.

Just as Abraham feared, Pharaoh, the Egyptian ruler, was indeed captivated by Sarah's beauty. As Abraham and Sarah had planned, they said they were siblings. Because of their lie, Pharaoh took Sarah into his palace intending to make her his wife.

What was Abraham's focus during this incident? He was worrying about his own life because his focus was on Sarah's beauty and the desire and strength of the Egyptian men. Abraham's anxiety about his inability to save himself gave birth to a fear that urged him to doubt the protection God offered. Instead of looking at the Promise Keeper, he focused on the wrong things, and as a result fear governed the way he functioned. Fear controlled his mind, his decisions, and his actions, and so he lied and encouraged his wife to lie as well.

Have you ever been there yourself? I personally have no room to talk about Abraham. As I dealt with the disabling effects of disease, I became afraid. Because I did not know how the Lord would provide a good job, favor with an employer, or a good mate, I felt the need to make myself appear to be a *"totally able-bodied woman!"* Honestly, it didn't work very well at all. But true to his great mercy and compassion, our all-powerful God intervened in my life.

God also came to Abraham's aid, and as a result Pharaoh found his household under many plagues. When Pharaoh finally realized Sarah was Abraham's wife, he expressed his frustration that they had been dishonest and that their lie caused the trouble occurring within the palace. He then commanded them to leave. And so they journeyed back to Canaan with the sheep, oxen, and cattle Pharaoh had given them.

God had intervened on Abraham's behalf in a miraculous way! The Lord blessed the couple despite their lies and unbelief and removed them from a tense situation. God stepped in because he had a plan that no one would be able to disrupt—delay, maybe, but not disrupt.

Abraham succumbed to fear when his view of man became greater than his view of God. If we are honest with ourselves, it is no different with us. When we allow anything to become magnified in our minds until it seems larger than God, our actions will not flow out of faith; instead they will be governed by fear. We will believe what we *think* man can do to us more than we believe what God has *promised* to do for us.

> For [God] Himself has said, "I will never leave you nor forsake you." So we may boldly say: "The LORD is my helper; I will not fear. What can man do to me?"
>
> —Hebrews 13:5-6

Second mistake

In an effort to "help" God do what he himself had promised to do, Abraham and Sarah made a bigger mess of things. Sarah had a plan to assist the sovereign God of the universe (Genesis 16). She reasoned that if Abraham would have a child with her maidservant, Hagar, the problem of an heir would be solved. Sarah, not believing in her heart what God had said he would do, felt certain that she was too old and would never be able to bear a son. Even though the Lord had already identified Abraham as the father and Sarah as the mother, *she* figured her seventy-six-year-old body was dead. So Abraham consented and created a son with Hagar—Ishmael.

The messes we make when we don't walk in faith! The question that plagued the mind of Sarah and Abraham was, *how?* When they couldn't figure out how God would do what he said he would do, they found a way that *they* figured would work. But years later Ishmael would challenge the promised son that came from Sarah's womb, beginning a chain of events that has led to chaos, confusion, and war that today plagues not only the Middle East but the rest of the world.

As God's children, we must never attempt to create solutions to problems only God can solve, nor try to find answers to questions that God alone can answer. In the end fabricated answers and solutions will always be more costly than time spent waiting on God.

As we can readily see, the consequences of Abraham's diversions from faith became more devastating and costly as he grew in the knowledge of God, and the same is true with us today. As we grow in the knowledge of God, so much more is required. Luke 12:48 tells us that "everyone to whom much is given, from him much will be required; and to whom much has been committed, of him they will ask the more."

Abraham's success: walking by faith

Abraham was one hundred years old and Sarah was ninety when she gave birth to Isaac, beginning the fulfillment of God's promise that through Abraham all nations would be blessed. After all their doubts, fears, and unbelief, and even after the terrible sin that resulted in the birth of Ishmael, God still kept his promise.

This next episode in Abraham's life (as recorded in Genesis 22) demonstrates why it is so important to know the Lord's character and to look through eyes of faith, for God made what must have seemed a very strange request of Abraham. He told Abraham to take his son—the very son that would continue the promise—and offer him as a burnt offering! On the surface it appeared that God was withdrawing his promise . After all, if Isaac were dead, the blessing of many descendants coming through him wasn't going to happen.

But instead of arguing or pleading, Abraham hurried to obey God, and in doing so displayed faith in several ways. The next morning, father and son began their journey together to the place where Isaac was to be sacrificed. Abraham told his servants to wait while he took Isaac up the mountain and that he and Isaac would return after worshipping (v. 5). He said this to them in faith because God had told him that Isaac was to be sacrificed. Hebrews 11:17-19 tells us exactly what Abraham was thinking: His faith at this point had become so strong, he reasoned that God was able to raise Isaac from the dead. Because Abraham knew God, he obeyed and stood firm on God's promises. He did not fear—he believed.

On the mountain, Isaac asked about the missing sacrificial lamb. In faith, Abraham responded by saying that the Lord would provide the sacrifice himself. As Abraham was preparing to kill Isaac, the angel of the Lord stopped him and provided a ram in the bushes for the sacrifice.

This is a far cry from the man who lied and asked his wife to lie by saying she was his sister. There was no sign of the man who had attempted to help God complete his plan by fathering a son with Hagar.

God tested Abraham on the mountain to prove his love for the Lord, his fear *of* the Lord, and to show how true obedience responds to commands that don't make sense. Since God is omniscient (all knowing), he knew how Abraham would respond. Because nothing surprises the Lord, I believe that one of the many reasons the Lord allowed this test in Abraham's life was to set an example for other children of God.

In the same way, we too may turn away from obeying and trusting the Lord. However, the Lord has not changed, and reaping consequences for disobedience remains the same. Therefore, our journey toward trust and obedience will be long and painful if we insist on working out the issues of life our way and continue to resist trusting God. When we trust and function in faith, the blessings that await us will be abundant!

The heart of God

Sacrificing Isaac was a test. *Every* child of God will be tested. The Lord wants to bless all his children, but our blessings are intimately intertwined with our obedience.

Abraham responded throughout this entire trial with total trust and faith in who God is and what God can do. The reward for this act of faith was an over-abundant blessing from the Lord that can be found in Abraham's innumerable descendants today.

The Lord had a plan for Abraham that did not change because of Abraham's unbelief and disobedience. God gave Abraham numerous opportunities to act in obedience. His previous failures did not mean God had lost patience with him, nor did it mean he was looking for a replacement. Repeated failures simply meant delayed fulfillment of God's promises.

It is believing in the Lord that makes men and women righteous in God's eyes, not the absence of mistakes (Genesis15:5; Romans 4:3). If Abraham had done the right thing for the wrong reason, or if he had done all of the right things without trusting in God, his actions would have been rendered either powerless or precarious. Hence, Abraham never would have been righteous in God's eyes.

What about you? What about me?

Now ask yourself this question: *Where am I in this Abrahamic faith process?* We may be at a point where we are denying that God is able to do what he has promised. We may admit that while he is able, he is not moving fast enough, and as a result we try to help him out. Or we may be in the place of total surrender, being still and watching our Lord work out his perfect plan. Maybe you are somewhere in between these stages, wavering back and forth.

Great comfort can come from what we have seen about God in Abraham's life. Despite Abraham's mistakes (only a couple have been mentioned here), God never changed; neither did his plans, purposes, and promises. The Lord will not change in his plans for you or for me! He shows the same mercy, grace, judgment, and love to each of his children. To please God, we must walk in faith, and the motive of our hearts must be pure.

I have caused myself a lot unnecessary pain and misery because I chose to do what seemed logical to me. Instead of trusting the Lord and being obedient to the Word of God, I have resisted the command to sacrifice my "Isaac." O the joy and blessing that could be ours if we would only model Abraham, our father, and walk in obedient faith, trusting the Lord wholeheartedly!

What to do when we fall

We all fall, but Psalm 37:23-24 assures us that the Lord orders our steps and delights in our way; therefore when we fall, we are not down and out. Look at Abraham. He didn't do it all right; he made mistakes. But he was a friend of God, highly favored in God's eyes. Every time he fell, he got up, sought forgiveness from God, and continued to walk in obedience. As we grow in Christ, knowing him more intimately, we too will mature, finding that we fall less often and get up quicker when we do. We don't stay down.

When I set out for Wright State University in Ohio, I had extremely limited vision and mobility and was far away from friends and family. The only one I had to trust was Jesus. It was clear to me, however, that grad school was the direction that he wanted me to go, so I had to trust him. But even with a declining health condition, I experienced the victory that results from walking by faith.

Now I understand that the Lord is all I need to go through the challenges I face in life. I have learned that victory cannot be earned, nor is it given when I function in fear. Victory is given when I function in faith. The lives of patriarchs in the Bible like Abraham demonstrate this to all of us. I have learned that whether times are good or bad, easy or difficult, happy or sad, I must trust the Lord and function in faith.

In the same way, God has a plan for your life. He has promises and a plan that he is eagerly waiting to fulfill. We cannot imagine the blessings that await us when we obey, but we must take the essential step of obedience. Serving a promise-keeping, trustworthy God should make obedience to him effortless.

"Let me lead you. Let me carry you. You can't do this without me." God says the same thing to each one of his children. But do we hear? Will we obey?

Food for thought

> Though I have fallen, I will rise … the LORD will be my light.
>
> —Micah 7:8 NIV

> For though a righteous man falls seven times, he rises again.
>
> —Proverbs 24:16 NIV

- Can you think of a time when you have functioned in fear?
- What caused you to be afraid?
- Did you rise again? Why or why not?
- How did the Lord show you his mercy?

CHAPTER 8

Fear: The Root and the Remedy

Principle: Covetousness is the root cause of unbelief, worry, and ultimately fear. The remedy is faith.

We have seen how God responded to his children when their hearts were filled with unbelief and their attitudes were governed by ingratitude, discontentment, and selfish ambition. In our own lives it is important for us to be able to identify these attitudes, preferably before they grow. If we can identify the starting point, we can avoid the fear cycle.

Where do these attitudes originate? At the core of it all is the sin of covetousness. Covetousness will cause us to think we know what is best for our lives. It is the springboard for unbelief, not trusting God. Ingratitude and discontentment fall under the umbrella of covetousness. We consider God's provision and blessing insufficient, and our selfish ambition drives us to please ourselves because we think God can't or won't.

The first step toward victory over the fear cycle is to deal with the sin of covetousness in our hearts. When a coveting spirit is given free reign, fear gains a solid foothold. It is necessary to identify the circumstances that create an environment in which attitudes such as ingratitude and selfishness can breed. We also must recognize that such attitudes move us away from God's perfect plan for our life. Lastly, we need to replace the bad attitudes we've identified with those that are pleasing to God: faithfulness, joyfulness, thankfulness, and contentment.

THE ROOT OF OUR FEARS

Covetousness

Covetousness is defined in *Vine's Complete Expository Dictionary* as the desire to have more or to lust. If covetousness had a voice it would say, "God, if you won't give it to me, I'll get it for myself. I love you, and my relationship with you is important, but I don't think you understand. There is nothing sinful about what I want, so I will figure out the best way to get it for myself." When we look at the things, or "blessings," of others, we consider it unjust if we desire that same "blessing" and don't get it.

Underneath the umbrella of covetousness, you'll also find the companion attitudes of envy and jealousy. All three of these attitudes show themselves when we murmur, grumble, and complain. If your mouth, lips, and tongue are innocent of complaining and murmuring, is your heart guilty? The Lord knows all and sees all. If your heart is guilty, every part of you is guilty. If we allow the Lord to keep our hearts free of a coveting spirit, our mouths, lips, and tongues will have no reason to grumble, murmur, and complain.

We often limit our definition of coveting to wanting what someone else has. Coveting also includes wanting more, more, more! Perhaps God wants to give us what we want, but not immediately. In addition we might want our circumstances to be different, or perhaps we might want another person to behave differently, instead of wanting God's will. There's nothing wrong with having a heart that desires things to be different. The problem arises when we want better things more than we want to please and glorify our Lord. Beware! "I" is always the focus of a coveting spirit.

I desired health, independence, and a change in circumstances more than I wanted to please God. I would not have known this if he had not shown me what was in my heart. I had neglected to take the time to be thankful for all the Lord had done for me. In doing so, I was really no better than the children of Israel. Because I wasn't murmuring, grumbling, and complaining on the outside, I had deceived myself. Praise God that he loved me despite what he saw in me! He loved me enough to show me my sin and change my heart. When he showed me what was hidden within, I repented of the sin of covetousness.

God wants to give all of his children liberty and freedom. He wants to take all of his children to the Promised Land. Check your attitude and ask the Lord to show you all that is hidden in your heart. Be sure that covetousness isn't keeping you from all he wants to give you.

I have heard that the easiest way to learn is by looking at the example of others. Let's look at the effect covetousness had in the life of Abraham and then in the lives of the Israelites. By learning from them we can avoid its pain.

What did they want more than they wanted God? Abraham desired an heir more than he desired God's will and God's way. The Israelites desired anything that would satisfy their physical needs more than they desired God's provision in God's time.

How did their sin of coveting draw them away from God and his perfect plan?

Because he wanted the son that God promised, Abraham took matters into his own hands, which resulted in the birth of Ishmael. However, God did make good his promise in his time, and Sarah gave birth to Isaac.

The children of Israel cried for freedom from their bondage in Egypt, and God released them. But even though God provided for their every need, they murmured and complained because they always wanted something else. As a result they spent forty years wandering in the desert.

How did their coveting affect others? The sibling rivalry between Ishmael and Isaac continues today. It is seen in the wars between their descendants, Israel (Isaac) and Palestine (Ishmael). In the twenty-first century the whole world continues to pay for Abraham's unbelief.

This trickle-down or domino effect is also seen in the lives of the children of Israel. The consequences were immediate in the lives of the parents and their children. Those twenty years old and above died in the wilderness and did not see the Promised Land. Everyone under twenty had to wander in the desert for forty years before entering because of their parents' unbelief. The Lord pronounced this judgment on the Israelites: "And your sons shall be shepherds in the wilderness forty years, and bear the brunt of your infidelity, until your carcasses are consumed in the wilderness" (Numbers 14:33).

In both situations there was a cost to them and to others for the covetousness that resulted in unbelief. The difference is found in the fact that Abraham grew to love God more, but the Israelites' growth was stunted.

Unbelief—a contagious infection

What the Lord has shown us in the lives of the Israelites and Abraham is still true today. Our personal choices, good or bad, affect the entire body of Christ. Are people experiencing blessings because of our faith and obedience, or are they bearing the brunt of the consequences due to our unbelief? It doesn't matter if they are family members, people in our church, or people on the other side of the world: Others reap with us, both the good and the bad.

Your adversity and mind-set

How many situations and trials do we go through in our lives where we focus on our circumstances? Instead of looking up at the Lord, we look around at our seemingly insurmountable problems. We choose to look at our circumstances, not at how our circumstances pale in comparison to God. Taking our eyes off of Jesus and looking down at our situation invariably leads to a self-centered spirit. It is sad to consider the number of victories and blessings we have not experienced and the people whose lives we have affected adversely because we focused on the wrong thing or things. Because of our faulty focus we refuse to move ahead in faith, which always results in us robbing God of the glory and praise that is rightfully his.

The Lord wants to be our all, our everything, our "enough." We need to recognize that God has given us much more than he gave Abraham and the Israelites. We know the resurrected Jesus Christ. We are recipients of his grace, and all born-again children of God have the power of the Holy Spirit of Christ living inside them!

We also have what those in the Bible did not have—the completed Word of God. This gives us an opportunity to look back and see how the Lord worked in the lives of his children in the past. Knowing how he worked then shows us how he desires to work in our lives today.

God is a gentleman: He never shows up without an invitation. You must invite him in. You need to ask Jesus to reside in your heart and set your circumstances in order. Then allow him to work in your life the way he chooses.

THE REMEDY FOR OUR FEARS

Gift from God

The only control we have over our fear is our response. We cannot prevent fear from coming. But the Lord has provided for sinful mankind what we could not provide for ourselves. Obeying the Lord and trusting him can remove all fear. For instance, when in a dark room or walking down a dark alley alone, you are unable to stop your rapid heart rate. But once you begin to remind yourself of a loving heavenly Father and his promises of protection, your heart rate can slow down. A heart-trust must accompany head-knowledge if we plan to conquer our fears.

The Person who truly and effectively gives us peace and confidence in the middle of a troubling situation is the Lord: "It is I; do not be afraid" (Matthew 14:27). But we will never experience the peace and contentment he longs to give us until we trust him and believe he is and always will be faithful to us. "Do not be afraid; only believe.... My peace I give to you.... Let not your heart be troubled, neither let it be afraid" (Luke 8:50; John 14:27). These are the words of the Lord Jesus Christ. Do we believe him?

The Choice

In Psalm 31 David recounted many of the problems he was facing. His solution was to turn to God: "In You, O LORD, I put my trust" (v. 1). He went back to the one true Source of deliverance. He had a choice to make, and each of us will have an opportunity to make the same choice: Do we dwell on our fears, or do we choose to trust?

This dilemma is the reason it is so important to become intimately acquainted with the person of God, the character of God, and the promises of God. How can we trust someone we do not know? How can we know someone we don't spend time with? If we don't do these two very necessary things, we are not going to be able to rest on his promises.

Peter, a man who took his eyes off Jesus many times, encourages us to "grow in the grace and knowledge of our Lord and Savior Jesus Christ" (2 Peter 3:18). In Isaiah 40:28 the Lord says to the bewildered children of Israel, "Have you not known? Have you not heard? The everlasting God, the Lord, the Creator of the ends of the earth, does not faint or grow weary." Regardless of our faithlessness and unbelief, the Lord will remain faithful.

He desires to use the hard times, the trials and testings, to take us to the next level in him—a deeper level! These are opportunities to go deeper in our knowledge of him, deeper in faith, and deeper in our intimacy with our Lord. God called Abraham from Ur and took him to Canaan. In the same way, God wants to take us from where we are right now to where he wants us to be. But like Abraham, we must be obedient to the Lord. We must be obedient to *everything* that he commands us to do.

> Have mercy on me, O LORD,
> for I am in trouble;
> My eye wastes away with grief,
> Yes, my soul and my body!
>
> For I hear the slander of many;
> Fear is on every side;
> While they take counsel together against me,
> They scheme to take away my life.
>
> But as for me, I trust in You, O LORD;
> I say, "You are my God."

My times are in Your hand;
Deliver me from the hand of my enemies,
And from those who persecute me.

—Psalm 31:9, 13–15

The Lord has made every provision for us and done much more than we deserve. Now we have to make the choice to trust. Trust is what saved the psalmist King David. He chose to divert his focus from his fears to his God, the one and only true God.

From fear to faith

As we prepare to shift our focus from fear to faith, it might be helpful to look at the Greek translations in *Strong's Concordance* for *trust, believe,* and *faith:* [4]

1. *trust* [Gr. peitho #3982]: agree, assure, believe, have confidence, be (wax) confident, make friends, obey, persuade, trust, yield.

2. *believe* [Gr. pisteuo #4100]: to have faith (in, upon, or with respect to, a person or thing), i.e. credit; by implication, to entrust (especially one's spiritual well-being to Christ):—believe(-r), commit (to trust), put in trust with.

3. *faith* [Gr. pistis #4102]: assurance, belief, believe, faith, fidelity.

These three words are closely related. There are small differences, but they have meanings that are very similar, if not identical. Trusting, having faith, believing. It may sound easy, but the work comes when we need to make a decision to put them into action. Just trust. Really believe. Have faith.

Believing is putting faith into action. We can say we believe in something, but unless we act on our belief, it is empty; it has no meaning; it does us no good. In the same way, we must not only understand that the Lord will be our strength and help us overcome life's struggles, but we must also let him do it!

The Lord desires that his children trust him and be obedient. He does not condone our unbelief and disobedience, but he is willing to forgive. He will forgive all of our mistakes. He gives the grace and the strength to endure. In that strength we must rise after we fall and then continue on in obedience. But we must believe that Jesus meant it when he said, "My grace is sufficient for you, for My strength is made perfect in weakness" (2 Corinthians 12:9).

A lesson

Since I became aware of fear and the role it has played in my life, the Lord has given me numerous opportunities to take the high road of faith. Looking into the lives of both Abraham and the Israelites, I became more aware of the choices that break the heart of God.

Since I know that fear brings about failure, and faith is the only response that pleases the Lord, the Lord has given me many opportunities to choose faith. One of those occasions was my response to the death of my mother. Another was my response to the debilitating nature of MS, and a third was the choice I've made after looking at the pruning of relationships in my life.

At the age of fifty-nine, Daisy Ross went home to be with Jesus after battling cancer for two years. My mother loved the Lord immensely and loved her family too. She was my teacher, my example, my stability, and my best friend—although I did not know it at the time. Her love for her family led her to shield us from the imminence of her death. She kept it to herself as long as she could because she did not want those around her spending her remaining days in mourning.

After I found out she was being called home and that she knew it, I realized there was nothing I could do to change things. My fear said, *I will try to help her get healed*—just as I had tried to fix my MS. However, the Bible said, "Trust in the LORD with all your heart, and lean not on your own understanding" (Proverbs 3:5). I had a choice, and I chose to believe the Lord. Psalm 92:15 says, "The LORD is upright; He is my rock, and there is no unrighteousness in Him."

Even though I didn't understand it, I knew God is right in everything he does. And the healing in my life that this knowledge brought then continues, even to this day. I have MS, and my mother is gone, but Jesus lives in my heart and comforts me every step of the way. Despite the adversity, he gives purpose and meaning to my life. I can rejoice as Paul did in 2 Corinthians 12:10, "When I am weak, then I am strong."

More lessons

Many years ago now, as my MS became more debilitating and my nerves became less able to transmit signals, I came to a place where I was unable to get into and out of bed without losing my balance. I was very frustrated and sad. I had gone from teaching aerobics, playing basketball, running track, and lifting weights to not being able to get my own body out of bed, and often losing my balance and falling while just trying to walk.

I struggled and I cried. Then I got angry with the Lord because it didn't make sense to me. I didn't understand why this had to happen, and I began to lose hope.

However, in this darkest time I still knew deep down that the Lord was the only hope I had. I had a choice to make, and so I chose to believe what God said in Psalm 145:14 (KJV): "The Lord upholdeth all that fall, and raiseth up all those that be bowed down."

When I surrendered to God, I was filled with peace and joy; I no longer had a hopeless outlook on life. I am so encouraged right now, even as I work on this book. I am reassured that God has a plan that will glorify himself through my life.

The third lesson learned was when the Lord put his finger on a personal relationship in my life. I felt the Lord had ordained that relationship, but he continually brought me back to the words of Jesus in John 15:2 (KJV):

> Every branch in me that beareth not fruit he
> taketh away: and every branch that beareth fruit,
> he purgeth it, that it may bring forth more fruit.

I had begun to fear that the Lord was going to take this person who had become so dear to me out of my life, and it soon became clear that he did indeed want me to sever that relationship. I struggled with his decision at first, but as time went by I began to see things from God's perspective. I just needed to get out of the thick of that relationship and trust in Jesus to work it all out. I was being pruned by the master Gardener, and in his wisdom he moved me from fear to faith.

Even in the best of relationships there has to be a purging process. God wants everything in our life to bear much fruit. Those things that do bear fruit now, God wants to bear even more—so there must be pruning. God has shown me that even if it's good, it can always be better. And whatever he wants in or out of our life, he is sovereign and is doing both what is best for us and what will ultimately glorify him. It's always better when we walk by faith and trust in the Lord.

Successful suffering

Making the choice to operate in faith instead of fear is the first step to living a life that is pleasing to God. Faith is the substance of things hoped for, the evidence of things unseen. Faith, even as small as a mustard seed, gives us as believers the power to move mountains. Praise God for faith! Know that he has wonderful blessings and a perfect plan for your life. But be certain of this: The times of testing and pruning will come along with them.

Many times our emotions and thoughts will clearly indicate to us whether we are functioning in fear or functioning in faith. Here are two questions to help identify which one motivates your actions:

- Do your hands reach out in an effort to control other people and your circumstances, or do they reach up, surrendered and submitting to God?

- Where are your eyes focused—on your circumstances or your Lord?

There will always be an opportunity to make a choice between fear and faith. The choice you make will be determined by your attitude and perspective. Successful suffering will be determined when you decide to walk by faith and not function in fear.

We all need to trust the Lord, knowing that adversity is an inescapable part of life. The question is, will you fear first or will you trust first? There is a way that is best. Which will you choose?

Food for thought

> Behold, God is my salvation, I will trust and not be afraid.
>
> —Isaiah 12:2

> Whenever I am afraid, I will trust in You.
>
> —Psalm 56:3

- Are you guilty of coveting? What do you want for yourself?
- Will you allow God to enable you to take advantage of the remedy he has provided?

- Can you recognize the situations and attitudes that create an environment of covetousness, unbelief, or fear?

- Who will be a recipient of your consequences, good or bad?

- Do you long to draw closer to Jesus?

LOOKING AHEAD

We understand that faith, trust, and belief are the remedy for our fears and our failures. We know these are the heart attitudes that please our Lord. Faith in God must reign supreme over the people and things we love most, over our questions and doubts, and over our circumstances. Exercising faith allows us to receive greater blessings from the Lord, makes us stronger soldiers for Jesus Christ, and makes us bear more fruit for his kingdom.

Faith has a powerful and positive effect on the believer in the midst of trouble and adversity. However, the effect of faith can only be experienced when we choose to exercise it. Faith will make a change in the way we view God, in our relationship with God, and in the way we perceive our adversity. In our prayers, our faith will positively impact the life of many others. Walking in faith will transform the heart. Remember, God promises blessings to everyone who will trust, believe, and have faith in him (Psalm 34:8; 84:12; Jeremiah 17:7).

Jesus repeatedly criticized his disciples for their failure to exercise faith. It was then and is today rare to see believers who will have a conviction to trust God *wholeheartedly* even in unfavorable or difficult circumstances. But he commended everyone who demonstrated total trust in him and chose to walk believing in him. Looking adverse circumstances in the face and telling the Lord that you choose to believe all that he says—regardless of how hopeless things may appear—bring a smile to his face. This is the faith that the Father will bless. He longs for all of his children to live according to trust/belief/faith in himself, his Word, his promises, and his ways.

Successful Suffering: Walking by Faith is the next book in this series. In it we will study the lives of other Christians who dared to believe the Lord in the midst of adverse circumstances, and I will share how I began learning to walk by faith myself. As we study the Bible and learn how other believers have trusted God and walked by faith, we will be in a better position to make the necessary applications to our own lives. Our goal will be to take the *victorious* walk of faith.

Soon to come:

Successful Suffering, Part 2: Walking by Faith

ENDNOTES

1. Strong, James, LL.D. S.T.D. "Hebrew and Aramaic Dictionary of the Old Testament," *The New Strong's Exhaustive Concordance of the Bible* (Nashville: Thomas Nelson Publishers, 1995), 59.

2. Simpson, A.B. "Be not dismayed: for I am thy God." *SermonIndex.Net. www.sermonindex.net.* (May 12, 2011).

3. Strong. "Concise Dictionary; Greek Testament," *The New Strong's Exhaustive Concordance of the Bible,* 62.

4. Strong, "Concise Dictionary; Greek Testament," *The New Strong's Exhaustive Concordance of the Bible,* 69, 71.

CPSIA information can be obtained at www.ICGtesting.com
Printed in the USA
LVOW122351260911

247960LV00001B/1/P

(317) 872 - 6838